LANCASHIRE PRIVIES

LANCASHIRE PRIVIES

by

RON FREETHY

COUNTRYSIDE BOOKS

NEWBURY · BERKSHIRE

First published 1998
© Ron Freethy 1998

COUNTRYSIDE BOOKS
3 Catherine Road
Newbury, Berkshire

ISBN 1 85306 524 2

Produced through MRM Associates Ltd., Reading
Typeset by Techniset Typesetters, Merseyside
Printed by J. W. Arrowsmith Ltd., Bristol

CONTENTS

The author ready with his muck ladle.

FOREWORD

When I was first asked to contribute a volume to the publisher's existing series covering privies in the counties of England I wondered if there would be enough material to warrant such a book dealing with Lancashire.

I need not have worried; following broadcast appeals on BBC local radio stations and various newspapers, letters were soon pouring in. Many (indeed most) were humorous and original but it soon became obvious that there was also a serious side to this subject.

These days we all take sophisticated plumbing for granted but what did our ancestors do? There is lots of social history about food and drink but few accounts of the disposal of the biological by-products of these. Lancashire was fortunate in the sense that its villages could dispose of the excrement with some ease. It was simply spread on the land as fertiliser which is almost certainly the origin of the term 'sewage farm'. But what happened as the Industrial Revolution gathered pace? Huge numbers of people were brought from rural areas to work in the mills and the population of the cotton towns not only increased but was concentrated into very confined spaces. The toilet arrangements were not only primitive but later found to be dangerous and there were frequent outbreaks of cholera especially in Manchester. The appalling conditions hereabouts were vividly recorded in the novels of Mrs Gaskell, Charles Dickens and Charles Kingsley but also in the more politically motivated accounts of Engels and Karl Marx.

When we discuss Lancashire's privies we therefore have to reach a balance between the social history of health and hygiene and the ribald music hall humour. In a book of this nature it is necessary to use the correct language and not mince words for the humour of the authentic toilet is down to earth and in the old days this was literally the case.

I have two vivid memories concerned with the family privy. I was four, it was 1940 and we were experiencing the explosive impact of Hitler's bombs. Uncle Bob headed for the outside privy which involved negotiating the coal shed ('coil oil' to us), hens, rabbits, a pile of wood and the Anderson shelter which was a hole dug in the ground and covered with corrugated iron and earth.

Apparently Bob had settled quickly having lit an oil lamp to provide heat and light in the dark confines of the privy. Then came the wailing sound of the sirens; Bob rose sharply and upset the paraffin lamp soaking his shirt tail which then caught fire. As we were shepherded to the shelter Bob emerged shouting 'Ouch my arse!', which was still smoking. 'Has Hitler come?' I said. 'No' said my mother, 'it's Uncle Bob – he's set fire to his shirt'. 'Shirt be buggered,' he shouted, 'I've burned my arse!'

So he had and whilst we sat and cowered in the shelter Bob was obliged to stand and glower so to speak. After the all clear he was bundled off to the hospital. Many years later I was talking to a school friend who said 'Do you remember your Uncle Bob? He was in hospital with my dad. He got burned on fire duty in the blitz didn't he?' 'Yes he did,' I said, 'and now the old lad is dead and gone I can at last tell the true story of how his arse got burned!'

There is also a family story of my grandfather who sailed out of Liverpool for many years and who once paid a visit to relatives in Canada who had made a tidy fortune out of mining. Grandad remembered that the Canadians had an inside toilet which flushed and in the summer they ate their meals outside on a patio with barbecues being the fashion. 'Here,' he said 'they eat outside and shit inside. I think it's much healthier to do it t'other way rahnd!'

I'm sure that every family has some sort of memory about the good old privy or at least being given the unenviable chore of cutting newspaper into squares, piercing the corners with a knitting needle or a meat skewer, threading it on a piece of string and hanging the package on a nail at the back of the door.

It is the story of these tales which makes up the substance of this book; in some cases the informant is happy to give their name but others are more bashful and prefer to remain anonymous.

Inevitably, when writing about Lancashire past and present one bumps up against the 1974 boundary changes. In my search for privy information I have cheerfully embraced all that was and is a 'Lankie' location, and hope you will too.

The book is therefore an anthology of Lancashire folks' memories of lost loos and private privies and without their humour and history this book would not have been possible.

RON FREETHY

[1]

PRIVIES OF YESTERYEAR

One of the first people to respond to my quest for memories of Lancashire privies was Mrs Mager of Blackburn who sent me a dialect poem written many years ago by Mary Smith. Mary lived at Weeton near Blackpool where she kept the village shop for upwards of 40 years. She loved writing poetry and her work was read regularly in the early days of Radio Lancashire in the early 1970s.

SPENDING A PENNY

There's a little place at every hooam as nobody can do beaut
  [do without],
Thi may be rich, or if they're poor they need it there's no doubt,
Eaurs [ours] used to be up t'garden, reet on past th' rhubarb
  bed,
Wi' whitewashed walls, an' weel-scrubbed booard, an' t' dooer
  were painted red.

If them four walls cud only tell aw t'secrets as they knew!
'Cause then we often went in pairs, for t'seat hed hoys [holes]
  for two.
Eaur toilet leaves were th'*Evening Post*, alung wi' t'*Daily Mail*.
Cut up in six inch squares they were, an' threaded on a nail.

This little place had lots o'names – you'll know a few, I fancy –
Like th' WC or carzy, th' little house or perhaps Nancy.
Morgan's Dyke, Mi Aunty's or maybe Necessary,
Privy, Petty, House o' Commons and, later lavatory.

Th' Observation, some cawd it 'cause yo cud sit an' view –
A gret square hoyl were cut in t' dooer as t' sun an' moon shone
   through.
An' mony a 'Sexton Blake' 's bin read behint that little dooer,
But mi Mother knew nowt on't, or we'd ner o' read no mooer.

But things hev awtered – nowadays we don't goo out in t'dark:
It's built in th' house, wi watter theer, as saves a lot o' wark
   [work].
Of awt' new fangled things they've med for deying an' for
   weshin',
To hev a modern closet is I think eaur biggest blessin'.

Mary Smith's memories obviously went back to the days when villages such as Weeton were more or less self sufficient and the contents of the earth privies were carried to the fields and spread on the land.

A lady from Langho wrote of a keeper's cottage which had an outside bucket privy: 'It was emptied weekly by the Rural District Council who had a tanker. When this was full the contents were spread on a field behind the Black Bull alongside the footpath to Dinckley Brook and Aspinall's Farm.'

Alan Williams tells me that in the Hodder Valley in 1934: 'The smallest room was down past our house and barn and into a field. The privy was a small drafty building and the seat was a board with two holes. In the dark we tottered along with a storm lamp to light our way. When the tubs were full the soil was spread on the meadow to help the hay grow. This was then mown and fed to the cows which provided milk for us.' Who said that recycling was a modern invention?

My Langho lady proved to be a mine of information but she was also a philosopher and an historian. She told me that incorporated into the church at Old Langho were parts of Whalley

Abbey brought to the village when Henry VIII dissolved the Cistercian monastery in 1536.

'Why we didn't follow the example of them monks I'll never know. They had flush toilets in them days. You go and look at the abbey ruins. You'll find long drops with the holes still there and the muck fell down into the channels leading to the river. Don't tek my word for it. Go and look.' I did and she was right!

The late Jimmy Fell, the Whalley historian, told me that the monks had their own version of soft toilet paper – they used old cloths which were cut into manageable squares. These were probably burned in the large fire of one of the reading areas.

The same lady who is 93 years young also told me to visit the village of Ribchester hugging the banks of the river Ribble and

The remains of the Roman bath-house at Ribchester on the banks of the river Ribble.

to look for the Roman bath-house where she told me: 'You will learn a thing or two from them Romans. It is us wot was savages not them. They knew how to use watter.'

So they did and I examined the recently restored Roman bath-house connected by a riverside footpath to the Roman Museum which was established in 1914. The Roman system of ablutions is explained and not for the Imperial troops was the use of the then expensive paper which we now use and, thanks to modern technology, at a reduced price. The Romans used a combination of a bidet and a sponge mounted on a stick to clean the 'anal orifices' which seems to be a delightful phrase to describe the fundament!

My Langho lady had not quite finished and told me to examine Norman castles and try to work out how the Normans disposed of their waste products. Here there are garderobes which were rather like long chimneys leading from the bedchambers directly into the moats. 'You haven't ever seen a long drop until you've stood near to a Norman garderobe,' she said with a wicked twinkle in her eyes.

There is no doubt that the large country houses such as Towneley Hall in Burnley, Haigh Hall at Wigan, Smithills Hall at Bolton, Turton Tower at Bolton, Speke Hall at Liverpool, Rufford Old Hall, Gawthorpe Hall in Padiham, Samlesbury Hall near Preston and Astley Hall near Chorley to name but a few took more care over hygiene than did the common folk.

They did not like the smell of excrement even if they were then not aware of the health dangers associated with it; one of the important functions of the Chamberlain in a household was to look after the bed chambers and the chamber pots which had to be emptied. The Chamberlain, however, was far too important an official to empty the 'pysse pots and stoole chairs' himself and a menial groom fulfilled this task. Sometimes the rich would take

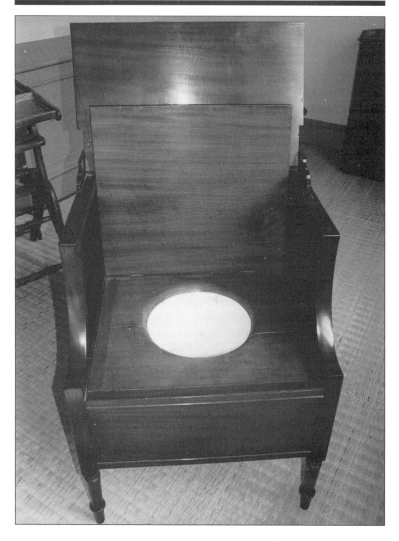

The Lancaster furniture company of Gillow made delightful and well-camouflaged commodes which were sold throughout Britain. This fine example is on display at Gawthorpe Hall near Burnley.

14

their chamber pots with them to banquets and servants would take away, empty and return these receptacles as and when required. It gives a whole new meaning to the term 'en-suite'.

In some of the rich households the chambers were beautifully handcrafted. Some pots were enclosed with 'close stools' which evolved into what we now know as commodes. To conceal their real function these stools were often richly draped in silk or tapestries; they would be emptied after use but at night pungent herbs were often burned on the fire to add fragrance to the bed chamber.

Whilst visiting 17th century Turton Tower (near Bolton) I noticed the door of what looked like a privy leading from the garden. It had not been opened for many years and after much pushing and pulling, entry was made to reveal a splendid three-holer privy. The Turton Tower Museum now intends to restore this and other privies and make a feature of them in the near future. Also at Turton Tower down one of its corridors and tucked behind a grandfather clock is a charming privy. Obviously separate toilets for visitors are not such a modern luxury as we might think.

In response to my search for privies in stately homes, I had a fascinating reply from David Chadwick of Gawthorpe Hall at Padiham near Burnley in which he regretted that there are no dry privies now left at the hall. 'But we do have a couple of aristocratic loos,' he said, 'one with a hinged lid and the other cunningly disguised as a bench. It was very much a case of out of sight out of mind when it came to bodily functions in Victorian times.'

Such luxuries would be denied to servants but ranks of wooden privy huts were often built close to rivers and small canals cut so that the excrement was flushed directly into the river. If you look at the design of any medieval town you will see that the rich houses were situated upstream for very obvious

15

The garden at Turton Tower and (*below*) the three-holer revealed behind one of its doors.

The delightful privy tucked away at Turton Tower.

An aristocratic privy in a wonderful state of repair. This is situated behind linenfold carving and is one of the many joys of Gawthorpe Hall in Padiham. This was the home of the Shuttleworth family and the hall was visited frequently by Charlotte Brontë, who must have made use of the facilities.

No. 20 Castle Park in Lancaster and the luxurious privy house which belonged to it, dating from the early 18th century. This gem still stands in all its glory. The entrance to the privy house can be seen, being the door on the right. (By kind permission of Lancaster City Museum.)

The charming rear entrance to No. 20 Castle Park's privy house. (By kind permission of Lancaster City Museum.)

reasons.

All capital cities expect to set examples with regard to the latest technology but when you think that in the 18th century there were almost 200 dwellings on London Bridge and for these only one privy was provided! You may assume that most people simply discharged their night soil into the Thames. What the facilities were in the rest of the country we can but wonder.

The poor old Irwell which flows between the cities of Manchester and Salford must have fared much worse than the Thames as the Industrial Revolution gathered pace and the river must have been an open sewer. Charles Kingsley whose fame is almost entirely due to his book *The Water Babies* also knew the industrial North very well and one of his poems is very evocative.

The privies at No. 20 were arranged at different levels; some for the family, with the servants having their own area. (By kind permission of Lancaster City Museum.)

Dank and Foul, dank and foul
By the smoky town with its murky cowl
Foul and dank, foul and dank
By wharf and river and slimy bank
Darker and darker the farther I go
Baser and baser the richer I grow.

There is a phrase in Lancashire which tells us that 'where there's muck there's money' and little effort was made in the cotton towns to implement the 1848 Public Health Act which legislated for 'the provision of an earth closet, privy, tippler bucket or perhaps a water closet available to every household.'

There was a loophole in the law which was not clear – could it be for each household or could there be 'shared facilities'? In that case one privy per hundred satisfied the law!

By the mid 19th century, not only were pawn shops reaching epidemic proportions in industrial Lancashire but disease was also rampant and a report on the sanitary conditions of Blackburn published in 1853 stresses that:

'Well-swept streets are highly desirable on the grounds of health and cleanliness, and imperatively necessary to the efficiency of a well digested system of sewers ... especially in courts and streets not declared highways, which are seldom if ever visited by the Scavenger ... This subject demands serious consideration not only on the grounds of economy and utility, but with reference to the effects it may have upon the residences adjoining the river, such as at Witton and Feniscowles.'

The report goes on to extol the virtues of collecting human sewage and using it as a fertiliser, quoting the work done by Professors Schubler and Hembstadt at the request of the Saxon and Prussian authorities. It showed that if a given quantity of the land, sown without manure, yields three times the seed employed, then the same quantity of land will produce as follows:

5 times the quantity sown when manured with old herbage.
7 times the quantity sown when manured with cow dung.
9 times the quantity sown when manured with pigeon dung.
10 times the quantity sown when manured with horse dung.
12 times the quantity sown when manured with human urine.
12 times the quantity sown when manured with goat dung.
12 times the quantity sown when manured with sheep dung.
14 times the quantity sown when manured with human dung and ox blood.

This report also indicates that most local authorities were prepared to employ scavengers who worked at night and hence they were often called 'night soil men'. The scavengers were not well remunerated and were usually paid by the truckload. This meant that the men elected to clear the easiest privies and those living around narrow and relatively inaccessible alleys either put up with the stench and vermin, removed the night soil themselves or bribed the scavengers with a few pennies.

I thought that finding illustrations of such scenes would be rather difficult but my friend Norman Young and my colleague Eric Leaver at *The Lancashire Evening Telegraph* located a photograph of scavengers hard at work in a street in Colne. This picture shows the old privies, the night soil cart and the scavengers hard at work.

Scenes like this would have been typical of all Lancashire

A team of scavengers at work in Colne around 1906.

This old mill workers' street on North Valley Road near Colne still has its privies, although the holes allowing access to the scavengers have long been bricked up.

towns for almost a century beginning during the 1830s and following requests from local newspapers I had more than 90 letters describing the night soil men. Without the scavengers Lancashire at work and play would have ground to a halt amid a slurry of sewage and the diseases associated with it.

To some extent improvements were insisted upon following the passing in 1875 of the Second Public Health Act by Disraeli's government, which at last realised that waste disposal was infinitely more difficult in towns than in the countryside. Lack of attention to such detail was bound to lead to large epidemics particularly of cholera and there would thus be a reduction in manufacturing efficiency at a time when Britain was struggling to compete with other countries who were catching up rapidly.

A report published in 1909 gives an account of the sanitary

conditions in Burnley, and shows that Lancashire was waking up to the problems of health and hygiene. It was reported that at the end of 1908 there were in Burnley: 6,840 fresh-water closets, 17,133 waste-water closets, 2,433 trough closets and 523 earthenware and pail closets. There were also 19,244 ashpits and 2,989 ashbins. Writing of these ashpits, the Medical Officer of Health, in his annual report for 1907, stated:

'The total abolition of ashpits with the defective doors and the consequent scattering of the contents about the street, and the nuisance which arises when these places are emptied, should be made the objective of a sanitary authority. An endeavour is made to lessen these evils by constant supervision. The ashpits are emptied as required, but as far as possible they should be cleaned out at least once a month . . .

'In the work of emptying these pits the refuse is thrown out of the pits into the street and then into the carts. In dry weather the refuse enters the houses in the immediate neighbourhood and contaminates everything within its reach. In numerous instances, where the houses are through houses with private yards, owing to defective doors or to the doors being wrenched off the refuse gets into the back passages and helps to choke up the channels and drains . . .

'Credit must be given to Burnley for adopting the waste-water carriage system at a time when most other Lancashire manufacturing towns were content with pail closets and privy middens. This was at a time when the town had not a good supply of water.'

This account clearly shows that some, if not all local authorities were tackling the problem of waste disposal in a systematic manner although until the 1950s there were no standard methods.

The invention of the modern lavatory seems to have come late on the hygiene scene and most would date the invention to Thomas Crapper in the 19th century. Not so it would seem, because the idea seems to have derived from the genius of Sir John Harrington. This influential gentleman was a godson of Elizabeth I and in 1590 he produced a flushing privy about which he noted that: 'The unfortunate sitter has invoked the devil by saying his prayers while engaged in less Godly business'. Sir John is one of many whose portrait is shown in the Oriel window of the Dining Room at Christ's College, Cambridge. He is in good company if we consider the biology of the privy because above him is none other than Charles Darwin. In view of the fact that a cornerstone of the theory of evolution was 'The Survival of the Fittest' it is a pity that Sir John Harrington's flush toilet did not catch on. Think of all the cholera epidemics which might have been prevented during the Industrial Revolution if the Elizabethan flush had been 'on stream'. If Crapper had not cornered the market the rude folks might have referred to going for a 'Harrington' rather than a 'Crap'. The word privy is also of interest and one dictionary definition gives 'Participating in the knowledge of something secret,' and then adds, 'a small lavatory especially relating to an outhouse'.

Few people seemed to be privy with the actual workings of the early lavatories but Albert Morris of Nelson was able to throw some light on the mechanisms involved. Many of the mill town rows of houses were fitted with a system of self-flushing lavatory, invented in the late 19th century. Situated in the back yard, they were automatically flushed periodically by an ingenious system called a 'tippler'. This was a very strongly built, thick-sided, open-topped earthenware container around two feet long, a foot wide and around ten inches deep and shaped like a huge shoe with a pouring spout where the toe would be and which would hold about four gallons of water.

There was a round lug at either side of the tippler, each of

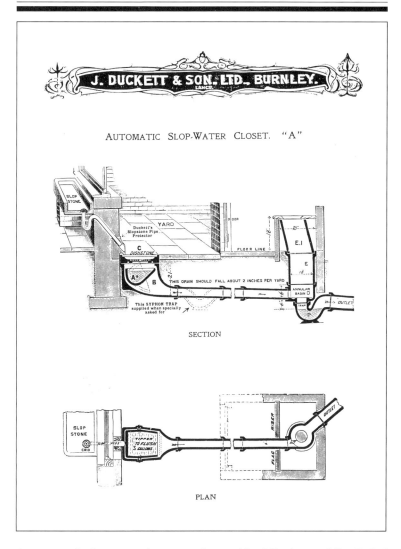

An automatic slop-water closet manufactured by J Duckett and Son Ltd of Burnley – this was the tippler system which recycled household waste water to flush the sides of a long drop privy.

which, fitted into half-round sockets, enabled it to see-saw up and down. It was built into an earthenware frame and the whole assembly was set in the yard well below ground level, to which waste water was conveyed by an underground pipe to fill the tippler when waste water ran from the kitchen sink or the 'slopstone' as it was called in those days.

Later ones were fitted just below ground level, underneath a square opening below an iron grating, where the waste water ran from the slopstone in the kitchen, through a short piece of lead piping into the backyard. Slopstones were usually a three inch deep, hollowed out slab of sandstone, some three feet long by two feet from back to front and were in use before more modern sinks were invented.

The tippler was made to be 'back heavy' and so rested with its back part down until the container part in front of the lugs filled with waste water. It would then become heavier than the back part and so would tip forward, emptying the water into a pipe which flushed the lavatory, situated some eight feet away from where the waste water ran from the kitchen. After its automatic emptying, it would take about five minutes to fill from a running tap and when it emptied, you could hear its loudish 'clunk'.

The lavatory in those days was called the 'long drop' as it was just that; the bottom being some five or six feet below ground level. It was constructed in the form of a stone-built tube some eighteen inches in diameter with a big rectangular wooden seat on top. Unfortunately, the sides of the long drop were not flushed as the flushing water ran in too low down, and so it often gave off a strong ammonia smell which made your eyes water, particularly in hot weather.

Perhaps with a little extra thought, the tippler system could have been better designed, enabling the sides to be flushed from higher up. However, they did the work reasonably well, removing waste matter and saving water by re-cycling it after it had

A tippler toilet actually operating in Chorley – very few remain anywhere in Britain. Notice the absence of a chain.

been used at least once before.

Albert Morris certainly had a point that many of the tipplers had design faults and many had almost a mind of their own as Mrs Renée Steeple who lived in Bacup told me: 'My great aunt lived at Waterfoot and had a tippler toilet close to the garden at the side of the house. I used to be terrified of sitting there with my legs sticking out and always shouted to my aunty in the kitchen not to run the cold water tap. This was the way that this toilet was flushed. On some occasions she turned the tap on and this caused bumping and splashing followed by the tippler depositing a deluge of water into the privy.'

Mr J. Hale of Chorley told me that his family had a tippler at the bottom of the garden and he was something of a practical joker. He could use a watering can so quietly that his young sister was attacked by a waterfall without her realising. One day his father watched the performance and waited until he was seated and then 'he gave me a bucket of washing-up water all to myself!'

Mrs V. Darlington of Accrington tells me that when she came to live in Lancashire from Somerset she was not familiar with the tippler system. Her first visit to a 'Lankie Loo' was in the dark and as she reached up for the chain she touched the tippler device and it operated in an uncontrolled deluge. She tried to do it again later but found that it was not quite so simple and got saturated for a second time!

Mrs Darlington also told me: 'Our family of three moved into a house with another family of five, all from Somerset. This was in Great Harwood and we were posh because we had an outside flush toilet which we were used to at home but at the end of the garden was a stone built privy. The two husbands decided to fill the long drop in using ashes from the fire in case one of the children got adventurous and fell in. The two men felt they had done a really good job until water started flooding down the side

The tippler toilet (see also page 29) which is fully functional and the pride and joy of Mr and Mrs Harvey of Chorley.

street. Neighbours told us that the waste water from the kitchen ran down a pipe into a basin underground which then fed by gravity into the long drop. The tippler arrangement kept the long drop clean. The husbands then spent ages with the children's buckets from our seaside holidays and had to make small shovels with long handles to clear out the ash and the water. They also had to clear out a lot of very smelly material from the days when the people before us used both the WC and the privy. It served us right for not asking for advice before filling in the hole!'

A report in the *Burnley News* records that on the 12th August 1933 there were still 18,285 tipplers in use in Burnley whilst the majority of buildings in Lancashire's villages were still relying upon the privy buckets which it has to be admitted were a great improvement upon the earth closets. The bucket however, was only useful if there was a reliable method of disposal. The Burnley Medical Officer of Health's report for 1972 says that even then there were still around 2,035 waste -water closets in Burnley (in 7% of the town's houses).

Very few people I suspect have been able to trace the history of the privy right up to modern times having taken a close biological and professional interest. One man can, however, and in response to a request for 'privy info' in *The Blackpool Gazette*, David Atkinson proved to be flush with information:

'Our privy was an outhouse reached through the wash house with a copper wash bowl heated over a coal fire. I also spent a lot of time before reaching school age with my aunt and uncle who had a farm. What a performance to reach the privy. We went out of the back door across a cobbled yard, up a narrow ginnel [passage], up some steps and across a paddock where we had to run the gauntlet of hens with an aggressive cockerel, not to mention the geese. The privy was semi-detached, both being two seaters, one for our farm and another for the farm cottage which

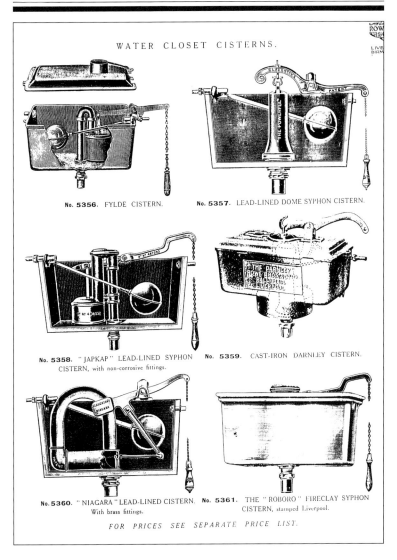

WATER CLOSET CISTERNS.

No. **5356**. FYLDE CISTERN.

No. **5357**. LEAD-LINED DOME SYPHON CISTERN.

No. **5358**. "JAPKAP" LEAD-LINED SYPHON CISTERN, with non-corrosive fittings.

No. **5359**. CAST-IRON DARNLEY CISTERN.

No. **5360**. "NIAGARA" LEAD-LINED CISTERN. With brass fittings.

No. **5361**. THE "ROBORO" FIRECLAY SYPHON CISTERN, stamped Liverpool.

FOR PRICES SEE SEPARATE PRICE LIST.

The luxury of the flush. Some fine examples on offer here from Rowe Bros & Co. Ltd.

was much closer to the business. Each was beautifully furnished inside and kept sparkling with whitewash, the seat polished until it was almost too slippy and the stone slab floor was always spotless. Looking back on it now our privy was stronger than most being constructed of solid stone and with a slate roof.

'Those of the village school were also dry closets but I can remember when the WCs were installed. What a treat they were. Some years later I ended up working at a plumber's merchants and over the years I must have sold thousands of WCs. Some names have lasted whilst others have faded into history which I guess will make your book useful as a bit of social history. What about Twyfords, Armitage and Shanks and Ideal Standard Doulton (Royal Doulton) which have survived the test of time? But who now remembers Howies, Southooks, Howson, Royal Stevenson and Royal Venton to name just a few?'

[2]

WHITEWASH AND A WELL-SCRUBBED BOARD

These days we live such sheltered lives (literally) that some of us only walk to the garage for the car whilst in the old days going to the toilet meant getting wrapped up in preparation for a long trek. In those grand old times it was often a case of running the gauntlet through the livestock and in the pitch dark.

Mrs Adamson of Wilpshire has clear memories of her grandparents' privy at Nappa in the 1940s: 'The toilet was across the garden about 150 yards away and up a couple of steps. It was a stone building (even the roof) and with ivy growing all over it. The privy was a wooden bench with a hole in it beneath which was a tin bucket. They kept geese as guards and we had to dodge these during our visits which were kept as few as possible. Just imagine at night when you were nice and warm next to the old black-leaded fireplace, closing the inside shutters, igniting a couple of paraffin lamps, their light revealing oat cakes drying on the clothes rack hanging from the ceiling. And then you had to go. Coat on. Umbrella ready if it was raining. Getting somebody to go with you to help dodge the geese. Going to the loo in those days was a scary experience!'

Jim Ashton of Huncoat, between Burnley and Accrington, told me of one unusual row of houses in Huncoat, known as Ormerod Row, built up against the eight foot high grass banking. Because of this odd feature, these old cottages had no backyards. To answer the calls of nature, those residents had to cross the main road through the village to the lavatories built opposite their front doors. Four more very old cottages, next to the White Lion Hotel didn't have any back doors, so a visit to the 'loo' for

Dean Farm in Great Harwood, taken in the 1960s with the privy on the right of the picture. Reaching the toilet at night was often a case of running the gauntlet through livestock in the pitch dark.

the residents, involved going round the block of houses, to the outdoor toilets situated around the back of their homes. This must have been quite a daunting experience for these folk, to leave the comfort and warmth of a cosy bed, to endure a visit to the 'petty', on a dark, cold, winter's night.

Mrs Coulson who also now lives near Chorley in the charming village of Withnell recalls that: 'When my husband and I were married in 1951 we lived in a gamekeeper's cottage – one up and one down and with a tiny bit partitioned off for a kitchen. The privy was more than 100 yards away and along a public footpath between Wheelton and Whithnell Fold. In the daytime we were greeted by locals who knew very well where we were going, which was quite embarrassing for a young lass. The privy was divided into two, one for coal and the other a two-holed long drop. In the winter my husband and I used to go together because I was frightened of this trek in the dark. We each carried buckets of coal on the return journey and how enjoyable it was, especially in the snow, when we took off our outdoor clothes, stocked up the fire and got cosy in front of the flames.'

Constance Jones of Blackpool has much less of a comfy feeling when she writes down her memories of a privy as a seven year old in the 1920s. 'I visited a friend who lived on a farm near Heysham and on my first visit we fed the livestock and were then given lots of home made lemonade and cakes. I was soon ready to go to the privy which seemed miles away although probably only about 200 yards. We had a "flush loo" at home and I was horrified to find a three-hole long drop. I opened the door to find two of the owner's sons busily engaged in "filling up the holes". I fled and by the time I got home I had wet my knickers. My mum was furious that I had not waited my turn or "done it in the hedge".'

These days it is the fashion to have en-suite combinations of bedrooms with private facilities. We do, however, often need planning permission to have such alterations done and we always need expert craftsmen to carry out the work. This was not the case a few generations ago when our homes were allowed to expand to cope with increases in the family. Eighty seven year old Audrey Miller, now of Wigan but who once lived in a farm cottage near Southport, told me that her 'father was crafty with his hands. When he was first married he built a lean-to privy with one leading down into a bucket. This he emptied on the allotment which he said provided the best possible strawberries and rhubarb. In the summer the smell often carried into the house so he then emptied the spoil into the river Douglas. Whenever he could he used to hang sweet-smelling herbs and flowers in and around the privy. I liked roses best but he also used a plant which I think he called mugwort. I remember this smell well because it reminds me of modern cough mixtures. When me and my brothers were born father increased the length of the bench and cut two holes, one for an adult and a smaller hole for a child. Until we were big enough not to slip through we had to go to the privy with an adult. We did not worry about privacy especially on nights when the wind was howling and rain falling with the candle flickering or in winter when an owl used to frighten us by hooting from its perch on the pear tree.'

These days we decorate the toilet as carefully as any other room in the house but this is not just a modern trend. Some used the long drop as a place of refuge and perhaps to have a quiet read. Mr McNamara of Nelson told me:

'We had a long drop toilet in the 1940s and granddad had it done up to add a bit of class to it. It was quite smart really to say that it was at the bottom of the yard. He wallpapered it and as soon as it went dark he used to light two oil lamps and the heat from these kept it warm. He also used to sprinkle bleach down to keep it free from bluebottles. He put a curtain on the window and hung fly papers from the whitewashed ceiling on a hook close to whilst on another hook hung the paper. He also regularly sandpapered the seat which he said stopped germs and also "splinters in our arses".'

Bob Hargreaves of Bury told me a wonderful tale about his

father who was a sailor working out of Liverpool in the 1880s. When he came back home to work at the shipbuilding yard at Cammell Laird he set about converting the privy into a memorial to the sea. Bob told me that the seat was made out of a piece of teak timber which shone like ebony and was so shiny that it was easy for small nippers to slip off. The cover was made from an old port hole cover which he said had come from a White Star Liner which had been broken up at Ward's Shipyard at Morecambe. Few privies had outside windows but grandad's had been made from another port hole with curtains of multi-coloured Japanese silk. These were a remnant of the textile brought back many years previously and from which grandma had made a 'posh frock'.

The walls of this temple of a privy were decorated with bits of marine debris, an advertising poster for the *Titanic* in 1912 and a framed newspaper article of the disaster. Most people were content with a nail hammered into the wall to hold the cut paper but not Bob's grandad. He had obviously seen some of the fittings on board liners and he had found a wonderfully ornate drawer handle made of polished brass. This was adapted to hold the squares of paper and in place of string was a long piece of scarlet silk.

Although Bob Hargreaves' story concerns a very special privy most people regarded the smallest room with the same pride as the rest of the house. Very few were filthy unhygienic fly-infested disease traps. They were usually whitewashed, scrubbed and manicured with the buckets or earth closets emptied regularly and the stench kept to an absolute minimum.

Some folk who were a little posher than the average decorated their privies by employing professionals. Alan Hayhurst told me of a joiner and undertaker who earned a good living from producing smooth wooden seats with covers. One day he had a burial to attend to and later in the day he had six toilet seats for delivery down the dale. His hearse was driven by two black stallions which walked slowly to the cemetery. He then delivered the coffin along with a huge number of wreaths and bouquets. Much to his chagrin he discovered that one of the mourners had seen the six toilet seats propped up behind the coffin and had 'used his nut'. He had the seats set into the fresh earth and used them to prop up the family flowers so that they stood proudly above the others. The bereaved were so pleased with the appearance that they spread the news and for many years the system became part of the undertaker's service!

These days we demand high quality homes, but in days gone by people were not quite so demanding as Muriel Little, now living in Rishton told me. She describes an idyllic childhood living with her farm-working parents between the villages of Twiston and Rimington on the slopes of Pendle Hill. The family home was a converted railway carriage which had been transported from the railway at Gisburn. The earth privy was at the rear which was easily emptied onto the vegetable patch which produced fresh food for the family. I'll wager that Muriel and her brother and sister had a wonderfully healthy childhood close to the disused lead mines and the village of Rimington.

Muriel's carriage memories brought in floods of letters and phone calls and another reader sent a photograph of a carriage home in 1975 by which time it was not lived in and it was almost derelict. It burnt down soon after. She recalls: 'Our family moved round the other side of Pendle to live in the village of Barley. At first we had to share a toilet with neighbours. Each family had to share the duty of scrubbing the board on which one sat. Later my father built our very own privy. There was a board or a door across the front which was lifted away to enable the bin to be lifted out and emptied. Once a week the horse and enclosed cart came round to empty the bins and sprinkle a pink disinfectant powder inside and then return the bucket to the pri-

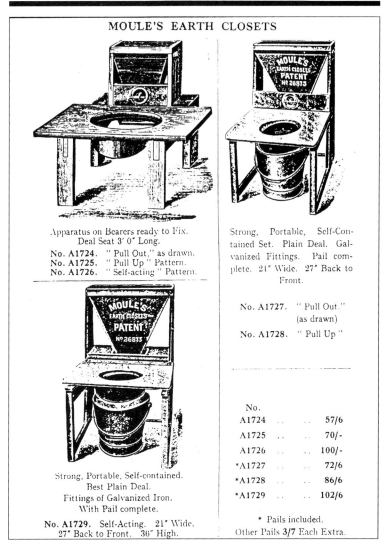

MOULE'S EARTH CLOSETS

Apparatus on Bearers ready to Fix.
Deal Seat 3' 0" Long.
No. A1724. "Pull Out," as drawn.
No. A1725. "Pull Up" Pattern.
No. A1726. "Self-acting" Pattern.

Strong, Portable, Self-Contained Set. Plain Deal. Galvanized Fittings. Pail complete. 21" Wide. 27" Back to Front.

No. A1727. "Pull Out." (as drawn)

No. A1728. "Pull Up"

Strong, Portable, Self-contained.
Best Plain Deal.
Fittings of Galvanized Iron.
With Pail complete.
No. A1729. Self-Acting. 21" Wide.
27" Back to Front. 36" High.

No.			
A1724	..	..	57/6
A1725	..	..	70/-
A1726	..	..	100/-
*A1727	..	..	72/6
*A1728	..	..	86/6
*A1729	..	..	102/6

* Pails included.
Other Pails 3/7 Each Extra.

First patented in 1860, Moule's earth closets were still popular at the outbreak of World War II.

A set of privies in Broad Oak Lane, the Nook at Staining, still bear evidence of past lavish whitewashing. In their day, they would have been scrubbed and manicured and the stench kept to a minimum.

vies. I remember one very young boy who used to ride on the muck cart with his Uncle Alf and the horse seemed to know just where to stand so that Alf did not have to carry the buckets which were often full and heavy. The housewives used to wait until Alf had gone and then the privies, pavements and steps were scrubbed clean. They used a block of sandstone which we called a donkey stone and which was obtained from the rag and bone man.

Joan Cirino of Huncoat also has a memory of the old muck cart and also of the primitive 'lavvy' of her childhood: 'It was rather like a long drop toilet with a wooden seat but with an inside which could be lifted out and was emptied once a week. Ours was ceramic and shaped like a very narrow dustbin. It was always emptied each week but if it was filled up sooner than that it was taken to the nearby fields and emptied with the paper being separated and burned. The man operating the muck cart used to empty the inner lining by hoisting it over his shoulder and he was very skilful in hurling it into the cart without spilling any of the contents.

'I was watching the muck man very early in the morning when I was too young to go to school and through the cottage window he mouthed: "I'll put you in if you like". Ever afterwards I used to run and hide on muck cart day and it became a family joke for many years. I can laugh now but it was a nightmare that tormented me every week until we went on mains drainage.

'Our father once had an argument with the next door neighbour because he thought that our toilet was filling up far too quickly and he blamed the neighbour for using our privy. I remember dad putting a lock on the door to keep the neighbour out. It was a real problem if you were taken short at night and the last to use it had not put the key in the right place.

'The cottage we lived in was one of four all very pleasantly situated in the countryside. The buildings, however, were back to back and we had no back door. The front door overlooked the privy which was next to the allotment. The lock on the door kept the hens from roosting on the seat. None of us children liked spiders so our mother had to keep brushing away the cobwebs but for some reason it was my father's job to dispose of the sticky fly papers which were hung from the ceiling.'

Joe McGinn of Blackpool has better memories than most of the earth privies which were very much a feature of the mill and mining towns of the industrial areas. Joe is a well respected artist and since 1993 has been a member of the Royal Academy. Joe told me that he called the privies in his district 'netties' and went on to write: 'Before drainage was installed these closets as well as being the only toilets were shared by several families and

43

ash was carried across the street to absorb the waste. It was not unusual for anyone "enthroned" to find the muck cart chaps shovelling away underneath them. Privacy at times like this was almost nil and small children were encouraged to leave the doors open so that adults could see that they were safe. The working miners usually had big families and small houses so they often took reading matter and a lamp to the privy and there they found peace with fact, fiction and a fag!'

Mary Thelfall of Chorley tells me of family holidays spent at nearby Whittle when their toilet was in the yard with a white wooden top with a hole in the middle and a tub underneath. 'It had a flap at the back so when the "muck drag" came to empty it, all they had to do was lift the flap. They disturbed people so often that one chap always carried a whistle like a football referee. He used to open the flap and deliver a blast on the whistle before starting his mucky work. This was probably more of a shock then hearing the scrape of the long-handled muck shovel.'

Mrs Conroy who now lives in Blackpool has a memory of when she was very young: 'My father took me to see my grandma and grandad in Penwortham. They had an old wooden hut for their privy which looked to me like a closed-in sentry box. When all their children were at home ten people used this. I was only three or four and I desperately wanted to use the loo. My dad was very proud of my sister and I and he told everybody that I was now old enough to go on my own. Horror of horrors when I opened the door of the privy and faced what looked like a big stage to me. I did manage to scramble up and face a great black gaping hole with a large bucket at the bottom of it. After studying the possibility of going down bottom first I reminded myself how clever my dad said I was so I gripped the edge of the seat until my knuckles were white and even managed to clamber down after. I think the memory of the praise I received outweighed the fear of my first encounter with an old privy.'

Mrs Ada Newton of Horwich near Bolton has fond memories of her 'privy days': 'I was born 17th March 1927 (St Patrick's Day). In the village we were considered posh. We had an outside water closet, whilst my friends had the dry midden type or the tippler closet. Mass unemployment of the thirties found us the same as our neighbours, poverty stricken. Strangely, I never had the experience of feeling poor, and so, had a very happy and contented childhood free of envy or jealousy.

'My mother was very strict; she was bringing me up on her own as my father had left us when I was three weeks old, to look for work elsewhere, he said. He never came back.

'My mother gave me the job of cutting newspapers up for the toilet. She gave me the scissors and a meat skewer to make the holes to thread the piece of hairy rough string through. When completed this was taken into the outside loo and hung on a nail behind the toilet door. But before I was given the job, my mother acted as censor and cut out all the juicy bits from the paper which she considered not fit for me to read.

'I remember to this day an article in the paper which was entitled "Murder in the cornfield". A picture of the cornfield with "X marks the spot" was alongside the story. The picture was allowed into the toilet, but not the news story alongside it, which was scrapped. Very frustrating for a good reader of my young age. Only when we were having visitors, perhaps our better off relatives, did we skimp and scrape to buy a toilet roll to hang behind the closet door.

'Our toilet was always spotless but it received an extra scrub of the white toilet wooden seat and the stone-flagged floor was donkey-stoned to a pristine whiteness.

'One such week-end my friend Jean needed to visit the toilet and used a piece of the toilet roll. "Oh! Jean," I said, "you shouldn't have done that, the toilet roll is only for visitors!"

Newspapers and comics were recycled and hung on a nail behind the toilet door. Those with pictures of Hitler were popular.

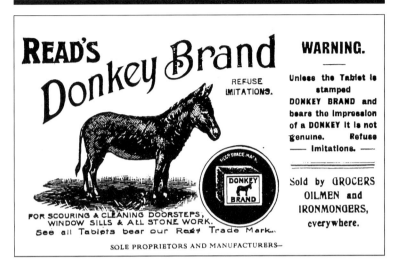

Steps were meticulously scrubbed clean with a donkey stone, a block of sand-stone obtained from the rag and bone man.

Jean flushed, then flounced off home saying: "Well, I'm a visitor aren't I?"

'Sixty years on in the supermarket check out queue I heard a voice say laughingly: "My God, you must be expecting a coach load of visitors!" I turned to find my old friend Jean laughing and pointing to the giant pack of toilet rolls in my trolley. We reminisced over a cup of coffee and returned home feeling thankful for the memories.'

Mike Wilson tells me of a story he overheard in a Lancashire market. A lady had bought four rolls of loo paper on a stall and was now bringing them back and demanding a refund. 'What's wrong with 'em?' she was asked. 'Nowt,' came the reply, 'but the posh friends we was expecting never turned up and we can't afford 'em ourselves.'

Mary Anderson of Wheelton near Chorley tells me that she

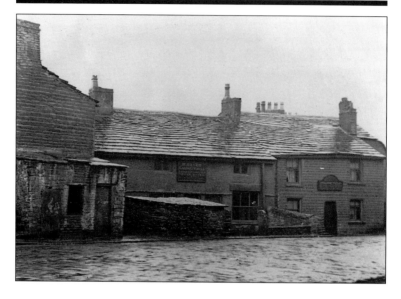

These public privies (seen on the left) were on the main road and were cleaned regularly by the council but the people in the side streets had to make their own arrangements. This scene in Oswaldtwistle near Accrington changed in 1915 when the Carnegie Library was built. The inn and cabinet maker's shop were demolished along with the privy.

still lives in the house in which she was born. Her trek to the privy seems to have been something of an obstacle course:

'There were steps down to the "backs" as we called them. Across the back was a petty [loo] which was semi-detached; one half was ours and the other belonged to next door. They were built of very solid stone and inside was a wooden seat with a tin bucket underneath. There was a door at the side which opened to allow the man who came with a "muck drag" as we called it to pull out the bucket. He used to put the muck on the fields. We used to take a shovel full of cold ash from the fire to put on the mess when we had finished. In the summer we used to add rose petals to improve the smell.

'The wooden parts of the privy were scrubbed every week and the flag floor mopped. If any one of the family wanted to go at night another member stood with a candle in a jam jar or later when we got posh we had a flashlight.

'When my sister got married and started a family of her own she and her husband lived with us and things did get a bit crowded. If the bucket filled before the "muck drag man" came on a Friday our men folk operated a rota and went down to the fields to empty the bucket and spread it on the land. We still love this old house but of course our sanitary arrangements have improved a lot since.'

The response for privy tales from many Lancashire newspapers was impressive to say the least and one of the funniest came from Barbara Pickles of Nelson: 'One Sunday morning we all went to chapel and by this time my cousin and I were at the "giddy stage", being about eleven years old. The preacher got up into the pulpit and gave out the text for the day: "Go into thy closet and close the door." I have no recollection of what the sermon was about after that but I can remember being reprimanded for laughing'.

Barbara also sent me a copy of a typescript which had been in her family for many years and although she pointed out that it was not original it was certainly funny. I couldn't agree more.

THE VICAR'S MISTAKE

A newly married couple decided to buy a cottage in the country. When they left, after looking it over, they remembered they hadn't noticed the WC so they wrote to the vicar who had shown them over the house and asked if he knew where it was. The vicar not knowing the term WC thought it was Wesley chapel they meant and this is how he replied:

Dear Sir,

I regret any delay in answering your letter, but the WC is 7 miles away from the house. This is rather unfortunate if you are in the habit of going regularly. However, it might please you to know that some people take their lunch and make a day of it.

By the way it is made to hold 300 people and the committee decided to ensure greater comfort by installing plush seats. Those who can spare the time walk to it, while others take the train. I myself never go but my wife went 2 years ago and she had to stand all the time.

There are special facilities for ladies, presided over by the vicar, who gives all the assistance required. The children sit together and sing during the proceedings. Hope this information will be of help.

Yours sincerely,

P.S. Hymn sheets will be found hanging behind the door.

Home and church privies are one thing but I also had a sheaf of letters about the embarrassment felt by youngsters who felt the 'urge to go' whilst at school. This is the subject of the next chapter.

[3]

TOILETS WITH TREPIDATION

I started school in 1941 in a village in the Lake District which is now in Cumbria but until the boundary changes of 1974 was in Lancashire. My first memory was of the dreadful stench and hordes of flies which emanated from the boys' toilets. We had a long drop privy at home but it was a haven of hygiene compared to this hell hole. I sometimes wonder if we did not ail much in later life because we were exposed to 'vile organisms' at an early age and built in a natural immunity. I have to say, however, that you can give me modern toilet facilities any time.

A Blackburn man of about my age writes:

'I started school in 1941 at nearby St Leonards (near the Petre Arms not far from Whalley). The privies were really just over an open drain and were "sometimes" flushed out by the caretaker with buckets of water but often the solid matter and the paper were left, especially on the hot days. Even in those days some parents refused to let their children go to that school purely for the sake of the privies.'

In 1911 the old Toll House at Paythorne near Gisburn was converted into a school. Many of the parents were farmers and for many years they collected the children from school in the afternoon taking the privy buckets home with them. The contents were emptied onto the fields with the rest of the night soil. The buckets were then washed out whilst the cows were being mucked out and brought back clean when the children went to school in the morning. I am told that the parents did this on a rota system but this was not a chore, it was a perk in the form of free fertiliser!

It was not just the children who had to put up with pitiful pri-

The privy bucket. Note the handles either side for careful carrying when dangerously full.

vies as Barbara Riding told me of the time she was teaching at an Infants' school in Blackburn. The staff privy was the same size as those of the children. 'To accommodate adults the wooden seat was made thicker. The trouble was if you didn't get the seat on at the right angle, you had the added embarrassment of having to fetch the mop and clean up that which had run under the door and trickled its way past the children's privies!'

Enid Wadsworth tells me that her mother went to a village school near Barley in the early 1900s. The school had squares of paper and the children helped to cut the squares, but on their farm neither of her parents or uncles could read or write and there was never any paper in the residence. They had, however, a ready made method which was to have a supply of hay on the seat of the privy. Once used the mucky material was taken into the stable and was mucked out with the horses.

She tells me of a trick played by one of her brothers. The local vet, who was not a qualified man in those days, being best described as a horse doctor, had been to treat a cart horse and had rubbed the animal with a strong liniment. The lad used his bit of hay and then impregnated the next batch with the horse liniment. The result was apparently dramatic as his uncle had soon to dip his backside into the horse trough. The result was inevitable – the uncle's stick meant that the lad also needed to have his bottom soothed!

Audrey Smales of Great Harwood tells of her school days when the children were asked to bring their own paper ready cut. 'This was a problem for some children whose parents could not read, but we all lived close to the countryside until the town

Staining gala day in 1959, with the village privy situated in the background, to the right, with three sets of windows.

got built up. Most people used large dock leaves or grass which we dried next to the kitchen range.'

Modern plumbing came later than you might think in some Lancashire villages. Lorraine Pemberton told me of her early memories of the village of Staining near Blackpool: 'I went to Staining Church of England school in 1962 when I was five and I remember the outside toilets with some trepidation. The building was situated alongside the church and there was a privy block close by. This held four cubicles each with a bucket type privy with a wooden seat. I was sitting there one day and for some reason I fidgeted and the whole bucket tipped over and I fell over, covered in the stinking contents. The only happy side to this was that I was sent home and had the rest of the day off whilst my clothes were washed. There was a second incident because I was then so frightened that the other children would laugh at me to try to make my bucket fall over again. I tried to fasten the privy door so tight that my fingers jammed between the hinge and I lost all the finger nails on my right hand, but fortunately there were no bones broken.'

Staining in the early 1960s still had no flush toilets and every week the council waggons came – one collected the contents of the middens and the other emptied the privies. The household refuse was shifted by workers armed with shovels whilst the bucket privies were emptied 'by hand'. There were some earth privies which were emptied using scoops which the locals called shit shovels unless they were in polite company when they were called soil ladles.

Mrs Swinton who owns the Thornfield Caravan Site in Staining remembers that in the 1940s there were some caravans and some chalets with the demand for holiday homes close to Blackpool increasing following the end of the war. There was a small lean-to bucket privy for every unit and these were collected by the dustbin men every week. The arrangement was that a shilling was left under the seat of the bucket for the dustbin men. No detergent or bleach could be added to the excrement because this killed the bacteria which carried out the biological digestion. This was the case with all privies whether they were of the long drop earth type or of the later earth and bucket type. From what I gather from town dwellers not all worried about what happened afterwards and poured bleach into the privies to kill the flies. In the 1950s the caravan site had a septic tank installed and the flushing toilets set in a block must have been a real boon. Obviously buckets were still used at night even from 1963 when the site was connected to the mains. At this time, however, caravaners emptied and washed out the buckets and it proved that newspaper was not easily flushed away and 'medicated' toilet roll became the norm.

Audrey Hopkirk told me that she and her husband worked

Thornfield Caravan Site in the 1940s. Some of the caravans had attached privies that were emptied by the 'bin men' who were rewarded with coins left under the seat.

together at a Lancashire village school during the Second World War. 'Being the caretaker, Billy's jobs were many and various but he had the job of emptying the school bucket privies and he took great care to take it all down to his allotment. He separated most of the paper from the soil and this was added to his bonfire whilst the rest was dug in. I was the school cook and how hard we tried to give some of the poor children a good nourishing meal. I suppose I dealt with what went in and Billy was responsible for some of which came out, so to speak.

'Children and staff seldom if ever (even these days) talk about bodily functions but I remember the head teacher being quite pleased when we had a consignment of apples delivered just after Christmas. Each was wrapped in soft paper and this was a real treat for us all when it was hung on a nail on the door of the privy.

'There's one final thing which you have made me think about. Toilet seats were often designed with little tots in mind but with no consideration being paid to the distance between the seat and the nail on the door. After a number of accidents Billy made special holders for the paper which the children could reach.'

Marlene Jaques of Burnley remembered that in the 1940s if you wanted to 'go properly' you had not only to ask the teacher if you could leave the room but you also had to ask for paper as it was strictly rationed. 'On one occasion I had eaten something which had upset my tummy and whilst at the privy I ran out of my ration of paper. You can imagine how embarrassing this was to a six year old. Ever after that I never left for that school without a reserve supply secreted in the band of my knickers.'

Bobbie Hesketh tells me about the time when he was at school in Blackpool and how in the summer he seldom attended because he was too busy earning a good living. In the late 1940s people used to pour into Blackpool for the Wakes weeks which meant that the cotton workers had staggered holidays with some towns beginning in June, whilst others ended in August. 'I used to earn money by diving and bagging. We went to Derby baths and the holiday makers used to throw pennies and we dived from the high board to collect them. I also did a lot of bagging which meant that you waited for a train and carried visitors' luggage for a tanner.

'It was because of bagging that my dad had trouble with the privy. I worked it out that it was easier to do my bagging by using a cart. I got wheels from an old pram and some old fencing wood served for the sides. I was, however, short of screws and a hinge for the top which meant that I could have a flap to keep luggage dry. I took one hinge from the privy door and several screws from where I thought they would not show. One day when I was out bagging, dad was in the garden privy contemplating nature when a strong gust of wind blew the privy door inwards. This proved to be the last straw and the poor old chap with his pants round his ankles was smothered beneath a shower of timber and to cap it all the privy bucket fell over him. I did not tell him until his sixty fifth birthday when I gave him a present of an inside toilet and bathroom which he thought "wer reet swanky".

Joyce McLellan now living in Staining near Blackpool remembers her school days when privies were a problem but adds some early memories of 'being taken to a pub way up on the moors and whilst our parents had a drink we children sat outside with bottles of pop. Naturally enough what goes in must come out and we were duly directed to what we thought was a garden shed. Inside was a thick bench with three round holes in it. "The big one's for dad, the middle one for mother and the smallest for you," we were told. The smell in there was so terrible that we refused to go in and so by the time we got home we were so desperate that we wished we had risked it.

'We lived in Manchester then and we were so posh that we had an outside loo but in September 1939 the bombing was

'The big one's for dad, the middle one for mother and the smallest for you!' A grand three-holer earth closet at Crook Farm, near Glasson Dock.

imminent and we were evacuated to Lytham. It was late at night by the time we were allocated to our digs. One of the first things we wanted was to go to the "lav" and we were amazed to be given a saucer with a candle on it. This was lit and we had to shield it as we went down the garden to the brick privy. It had a door made of planks but with large gaps at the top and bottom and with narrow places for the wind to blow through almost everywhere else.

'The candle seemed to provide plenty of light and everywhere was whitewashed and clean as a pin. I was glad it was only a one seater because there are times when it is good to be alone and with the breeze blowing through it continually the smell was not so bad. I can still smell it though, if I close my eyes and think back to the war years. These privies were certainly a topic

58

of interest to us "vaccies" as we called ourselves.'

Lancashire more than most counties can provide a link between this chapter and the one which follows which describes privies in the work place and also in areas of entertainment.

The cotton mill towns had a system of half time working. Josh Armstead of Oldham who was 99 when he died last year remembered this system well. 'I were quite a bright lad and like four others in my class I passed what were called "the scholarship" but I could not afford to go. We were all hard up in them days and so when I were 12 I had passed to a grade when I could work part time and go to school part time. I had to get up at 5 o'clock before it were light to get to the mill for six. My dad made me go part time but he always made sure I had a big pint mug of tea and a slice of bread and butter inside me before I left for work. I were usually late so I had to run and by the time I got there I were bustin' for a pee. Privies were rationed and so were the times when you could go. I'll be honest – I peed in the grate before going in because the privies in the mill were smelly and the big lads used to play tricks on the half timers while we were in. Old picking sticks off the looms were very painful if they were aimed reet. They were made of hide and I remember folks used to tek 'em home for their dogs to chew.

'By the time we got to school in the afternoon I were so tired that I wanted to sleep. One schoolmaster, Mr Johnson, were kind and he used to let us put our heads down on our desks and snooze away quietly because we had already reached the minimum standard. The other children had to keep studying until they passed the grades to enable them to go half time in the mills.

'I never forgot how horrible those privies were and the first year I were married, my wife and me (she also worked as a part timer when she were young) saved up and did not go on holiday for Wakes Weeks. We then bought a proper posh WC – we felt like royalty!'

[4]

PRIVIES AT WORK AND PLAY

When cotton began to make cash the rush was on to build more
and more mills and to construct more and more houses in which
to accommodate the workers. Most of the buildings, including
the homes of the mill owners, were functional rather than fanci-
ful and little attention was paid to sophisticated sanitation.

It was not just the cotton industry which ignored hygiene as a
correspondent working in Darwen pipe works in the 1930s
wrote: "The toilets were a plank of wood about 8ft 6in long set
inside a lean-to shed. Cut into the plank which was about one

A street of terraced houses in Colne near the site of the mill which once
employed the workers, now demolished. The privy blocks can clearly be seen.

60

inch thick were about six positions with a bucket under each position. During the afternoon the strict boss used to send people to relieve those who worked on the presses and they used to go out to the toilets and there they would sit for no more than five minutes enjoying "a dump and a fag".

'If you wanted to make water during the day there were holes in the wall with a piece of channel pipe set at an angle and the water ran through the hole and ran down the outside of the wall. These we called bog holes.

'When we came home after the war it was still like that for three or four years until they built some proper toilets. Not bad don't you think for a firm which made sanitary ware? They never had a canteen or anything like that. You took your own dinner and either warmed it up on the top of the steam presses or on the boiler lid. I sometimes took some egg and bacon and cooked it on a tin or enamel plate on top of the red-hot fire brick kiln hole. Everybody knew if you had a stomach upset because nobody was allowed to have more than one "serious" toilet break during the day.'

Mrs Ainsworth of Blackburn told me of similar problems faced by her mother-in-law who died in 1992 aged 94. 'In her younger days she was a weaver at the Florence Mill near Shaw Bridge on Whalley New Road. For the weavers three toilets were placed together but without any doors. This lack of privacy was embarrassing, but the overlooker could ensure that nobody was wasting time. It was not until a lady factory inspector came to the mill that the manager was instructed to have doors fixed to the "necessaries".'

Joan Evans of Oswaldtwistle Mills was responsible for the setting up of the 'Time Tunnel Exhibition of Cotton' in what is now the mill shop. She agreed that doors on the privies came late and often there were only six units – three for men and three for women. There were 500 women there and the toilet facilities were governed by a tally system. Three circular rings were hung on a beam and when an operative wanted to go they took a ring and returned it when they had finished. If no rings were present then the weaver had to wait – it saved working time because the system ensured that there were no queues.

Dennis Davidson of Blackpool tells me that in the mills and other factories your time in the privies was limited. After a time the overlooker would shout at the numbered doors: 'No. 1 Wiping!' or 'No. 3 Wiping!' This meant: 'Get that fag out, use the toilet paper, put the newspaper away and get back to work!'

His wife Ann told me that in her Blackpool office the phrase for going to the privy was 'to wash your cup'. When someone was taking too long a voice on the corridor would boom out: 'Now then Ann, have you finished washing your cup?'

Jim Fallon of Manchester tells me that in his works, many men used the sanctuary of the toilet to write out their betting slips which were then handed secretly to the bookies' runner: 'These activities were illegal and the management were not happy either. We had one boss who peeped under the privy doors and shouted, 'Nobody shits with their ankles crossed! Stop writing out bets and get back to work!'

All the Lancashire cotton mills had rules which we would regard as draconian in the extreme and very much against the civil liberty laws we have today. Despite this, however, the Lancashire humour shone through and this was reflected in both the jokes and the antics, some obviously on the subject of toilets.

One of the most memorable days spent working on this book was during a conversation with Councillor Ben Wallsworth, an old time Salfordian. We talked about his joy at seeing Salford Quays revitalised with the plans for the Lowry Centre now well advanced and ready to welcome the Millennium. Ben's memory can also go back to another age when Salford Docks had more than its fair share of slums. He told me that 'the privy bins were known as "dolly vardens" and there was usually one bin for every four houses. When full they were taken to and emptied into a barge anchored alongside the Manchester Ship Canal. When this barge was full it was taken along the canal and sailed out into Liverpool Bay where it was discharged in the Mersey estuary.' He also enjoyed the humour that 'Manchester's shit was exported to Liverpool'.

'There's so much luxury now with what I call "taken for granted" plumbing. I'll tell you one thing though – folks could leave their doors open in those days,' he reflected, but then with a wicked grin he added 'but then we 'ad nowt to pinch – 'cept shit!'

A little while later I spoke to Mike Crabtree of North West Water (United Utilities) who told me that during the period of heavy industry the sewage overflow from many houses fermented in the drains especially in hot weather. As a lad he remembers making paper boats, setting them on fire and floating them into the drains. They were often rewarded with a loud explosion as the methane gas from the sewage detonated.

Jim Ashton of Huncoat remembers: 'During the mid 1940s, when I was working in the blacksmith's shop at Huncoat colliery, I wasn't at all happy at using the tub toilets. Two men came twice a week, with a horse and cart to empty the tubs, which were dragged out from a hole in the rear wall. On one occasion, when the wooden flap door had come off its hinges, one of the apprentice mechanics seized the opportunity to set alight a rolled-up page of newspaper and thrust it through the opening, frightening the life out of the occupant sitting on the lavatory seat.'

Hygiene was always a problem and this must have been a particular problem for the mining communities. Albert Johnson who is now 87 tells me that his father worked in the pits at Wigan and Leigh in the days before pit head baths were pro-

Communal privies were common features in mining and textile areas. The artist, Joe McGinn RA, lives in Blackpool and is one of the few accomplished artists who depict everyday scenes of the 1920s and 1930s.

vided. 'The old man once arrived home reet mucky but feeling a bit off and had diarrhoea. He had just settled down in the tin bath tub by the fire to wash the coal off when he was taken short. Wrapped only in a towel he set off to the privy which was shared by three other houses. It was nearly dark and he tripped up over a mop. The handle hit him sharply in the privates and he let out a gasp. Out popped his false teeth and fell down the long drop. He was so desperate he still had to go and when he got back he was in a terrible state. He was still mucky and had no teeth. Teeth were not cheap in them days so he sent me and my brother to borrow a fishing net. It still would not reach so we had to go in the dark to his friend and we borrowed a walking stick and fastened this to the net. He offered us a shilling to catch his teeth. I'll never forget the smell as we peered into the dark using only a candle in a jam jar. It took us ages but eventually up came the teeth. We got our shilling and also a fish and chip supper, with mushy peas as an extra reward. We ate, whilst dad paid regular and obviously uncomfortable visits to the privy but with his teeth left behind and grinning happily in a jam jar!'

Walter Houghton of Salford tells me that his grandfather 'made a bit extra' by locating lost items including teeth, rings and on one occasion a docker's wage packet which had fallen down the long drop. In the case of the wage packet the scavenger was called in on a Sunday as the family had no money until that which was lost was recovered.

Mike Crabtree who now works in an executive capacity for North West Water told me of the days when he was working in a sewage treatment works. He lost count of the number of phone calls he received from people who had lost objects down the loo asking if they would look out for them 'as they passed through'. Top of the list by a large margin were false teeth followed by engagement rings and on one occasion a wig!

Peter Hartley of Colne rang me to shed light on his 'long drop experiences' in the industrial village of Brierfield near Burnley. The house in which Peter lived was in a back to back terrace which was typical of cotton villages. This design saved on space but the two-up, two-down terrace with only one entrance must have been fairly cramped.

Peter Hartley's home had a long drop which was more than 20 feet deep and he tells me that his father used to pack snow down the drop in winter and as this melted it automatically cleaned the contraption. It was emptied irregularly by the bin men with a long-handled scoop which he knew was a filthy stinking job. Peter and his brother were given the task of whitewashing the privy and the drop. The privy itself was easy but the drop itself was treated with a long-handled brush.

During the Railway Age in the 1850s, planners from Derby built terraces of houses for workers at Carnforth. At Millhead, the old privies still stand but now function as outhouses.

'There was a hardware shop in Brierfield called Coupers who would hire out long brushes for 6d ($2\frac{1}{2}$ pence) per day and if you told them of items which had fallen down the long drop they provided an assortment of tools which could be used to retrieve the relevant item.

'Close to Coupers there was Whites foundry. When the time came to convert long drops to "proper toilets" not everybody could afford to convert. They did, however, market a funnel-shaped, enamel-lined pot which looked like a posh loo but in fact was only a cosmetic improvement providing a smooth chute down to the old long drop.' Peter, however, did point out that it was much easier to clean.

Peter also remembers that in winter a paraffin lamp was usually kept lit behind the door. This was not to prevent freezing

A paraffin lamp was usually kept lit behind the privy door to provide light and heat on dark nights and cold winter mornings.

up (because there were no water pipes in the long drop or bucket system) but merely to provide heat and light on dark nights and early mornings when folk started work early.

This brings me to the pride people took in maintaining a clean privy and some were obliged to provide the same facilities for their customers. Albert Gillings had a garage on Preston New Road and in those days a 'repair while you wait' service was offered. Mechanics in those days could set to with a lathe and produce spare parts which would get customers home. A privy was therefore an essential service for those who had to wait a long time for their vehicle. Business was brisk during the holiday season and, from the 1950s onwards, during the illuminations. There was even a sign on the workshop window asking for newspapers – cut up if possible!

On one occasion the road was being repaired, and there was the smell of hot tar and the belching roar of the steam roller drowned out the sound of traffic. During a lull from his own repair work and serving petrol, Albert went to the privy where he was greeted by a most alarming sight. There was a chap already in situ but he was jumping up and down with his feet apparently on fire. It turned out to be one of the workmen from the tar gang who had gone into the privy with hot tar on his clog irons which had set fire to some paper which he had knocked on the floor. This in turn set fire to his trouser bottoms which were impregnated with tar. Much to the amusement of Albert and the man's mates, the tar man fled to the water pump in the garage forecourt and was soon steaming with relief but this was offset by his embarrassment. Red legs and a red face were, however, the only damage caused.

This brings me to the subject of the paper used in the privies. Toilet paper although it was patented as early as 1880 was not extensively used until the 1930s and was only for the posh until the 1950s. All the modern felted treats were not for the privy or

68

early chain flushers but a product for the more delicate backsides of the 1970s onwards.

There is a tendency these days, especially in well to do households to provide humorous or even titillating literature on shelves in the toilet, but reading in the old privy was very much a temporary thrill. David Kerr who died in his 90s in the 1970s was a great friend of mine and he told me of his days as an apprentice blacksmith in a Burnley coal mine. The work's privy was of the earth type and it was his job to cover over the older workers' excrement by shovelling coal dust onto it. David was doing a little business on his own account and was sitting quietly reading the newspaper when he heard shouts from all over the pit to say that the *Titanic* had sunk. David pulled up his pants and ran headlong to spread the news when he ran into the hammer of a master blacksmith and David's right arm was shattered. He showed me the scar which was still visible and this lovely old man had the usual twinkle in his eye: 'Nineteen twelve it was,' said David in his lovely Scots accent 'and it was bad luck to be off work with no pay in those days but it was even worse trying to learn to wipe my arse with my left hand.'

Alan Postlethwaite of Clitheroe told me that he preferred *The Hotspur* which was printed on absorbent paper to *The Eagle* with Dan Dare and the Mekon which had much more colour but was far too shiny and slippery to guarantee a good wipe!

Dorothy Sinclair of Chorley remembers getting into trouble at her father's works for stealing. She had brought her father's 'bait' (lunch) from the cotton mill and been taken short. She had used the necessary, 'and whilst I was sitting down I started to read *The Beano*, which had only been cut in half and not in small squares. When I'd finished my business I stuffed the unread comic into my knickers not realising that there was no paper left. The lady who followed me had only just delivered *The Beano* but had been called away by a supervisor just before

I arrived. The weaver only realised all her paper had gone when she got to the wiping stage. I don't know to this day how she managed but when my father, who had a Lancashire sense of humour, came home he told me why he had had such a "Dandy of a row".'

Immediately after a live radio programme in which I asked for information about privies I had a phone call from a well respected lady GP. She told me that she and her brother were born on a Lancashire farm. In the early 1950s she had taken her storm lamp down the garden to the 'thunder box' and by the flickering light she read half a page from a magazine about birds. The article described how to mend the wing of a racing pigeon. She kept the fragment and showed it to her brother and for many years afterwards they tended wild birds and mammals. Whenever the vet came, the pair asked questions until he must have been tired of the two children. The lady is now a doctor and her brother has a large veterinary practice in Yorkshire. 'I suppose we've both been privy counsellors ever since I went down to the thunder box on that wet and windy night. I hope you found this of interest.' Indeed I did but I forgot to ask her opinion on why kids exposed to the germs rampant in old privies managed to stay healthy. There may be something to be said for inventing a new phrase: 'Where there's muck there's immunity.'

This pair were obviously hard working, but others were more mischievous and several of my correspondents tell me that boys were found lurking around the privies of the girls. They were very good at waiting for the lass to get started and then poking a long stick through one of the many apertures. To the end of the stick they attached a bunch of nettles, thistles or even a pin. This was one of the pranks played at village dance halls where the privy was invariably a lean-to shed only partly protected by corrugated iron sheets.

The toilet facilities at sports grounds are the subject of complaints even these days and I tried to find out what conditions were like just after the formation of the football league which was largely developed because of the population and spending power of the cotton towns. How do you cater for the natural bodily functions of more than 40,000 fans which swarmed into Blackburn's Ewood Park, Bolton's Burnden Park, Burnley's Turf Moor, Preston's Deepdale or Bloomfield Road – the home of Blackpool. The answer is that a rough shed was provided after which it was a case of out of sight and out of mind as long as you were not a member of the ground staff when Monday morning bog duty must have been a nightmare.

The facilities at cricket matches were likewise primitive but at least the crowds were not as large. The smell of the privy on a hot summer's afternoon, however, could be unpleasant and the buzzing flies were not to be recommended either. In one of the villages the local blacksmith served a treble function. Harry Burton was a demon fast bowler, whirlwind slogger and as near a professional as you could get. He was also the privy emptier which he was glad about – he added it to his allotment which was the best in the village. He was paid to do this and to white-wash 'anything which did not move' as well as to mow the wicket which he always prepared to please himself. He was the scourge of umpires and on one particular afternoon he emptied the bucket over the umpire's car and was heard to growl: 'I've bin listenin to thy shit all afternoon so I've given thee some o' mine'.

On a more serious yet equally fascinating note, Cliff Hodkisson of Poulton-le-Fylde told me that he was 'born in 1913 in Preston's Victoria Street which was a street of two-up, two-down terraced houses each with a back yard and an outside toilet. This was carefully whitewashed every year. My father was unemployed at this time as most cotton workers were and he used to scrape the whitewash off the toilet walls and grind it into a powder. The children then had to wrap the lime powder into packets made of scrap paper. Father would then go out at night and sell this from door to door as "Aspidistra" powder. I don't know if one of his clients ever grew "the biggest aspidistra in the world" with our home-made soil improver, but he always sold a lot and I'm sure it kept our family away from the pawn shop which was used so much in those bad old times.'

[5]

CRITTERS IN THE LOO

There has always been a warning in the entertainment business on the theme of never working with children or animals. This is probably because they often produce the funniest incidents. Mrs Greta Adamson of Blackburn remembers when she lived in Chatburn, 'where we kept a few bantams. The privy was in the yard and one night my mother went to pay a visit without taking her candle and soon she let out such a yell that we thought she had seen a ghost. She had almost crushed to death a bantam which was roosting on the seat. Guess where the bird pecked her? It took her ages to live it down!'

D. McNamara of Nelson, had a father who was proud of the splendour of his outside loo and 'even made a round lid with a handle on top of it. One day he forgot to put the lid on and one of our kittens jumped up onto the seat and then fell down. The poor thing could be heard crying and we had to lock the mother cat in the larder under the stairs or she would have been down after it. My sister and two brothers became upset because we thought Ginger would soon die in the long drop. We tried everything to get the poor thing up but all failed. I then asked my mum if she had any clothes she did not want. I cut these into strips, fastened them together and went "fishing". After two hours I felt the increased weight and up came a stinking kitten. Soon Ginger was washed, clean, dry and purring next to his mother whilst I was champion of the household for a day or two!'

Wally Marshal told me of a very crafty tom cat during the war in Salford. For several nights running German bombers wreaked havoc around the docks and on the first night Felix the cat was terrified. By the third night Felix recognised the warning siren

A lid like this one over an earth closet at Roeburndale could be a useful accessory. (By kind permission of Lancaster City Museum.)

and the family headed for the shelter whilst the cat was seen scurrying to the privy which was of the long drop type and he became a master at lifting the seat. It was easy to see how he got down but how he returned after the all clear nobody seemed to know. Later Wally joined the RAF as a rear gunner but he never forgot Felix. He told this story to the crew and on each of many missions over Berlin, flying from a Lincolnshire airfield into Germany, they dropped the contents of an earth closet which was carefully placed in a sack weighted down with a brick. This was added to the bomb load and the amusement no doubt helped to dispel the fear in the airmen. After the war and

74

no doubt in remembrance of the Dam Busters, Felix's replacement after nearly 20 years of active service was named 'Barnes Wallis'. One of her kittens was called Adolf.

Mrs V. Darlington of Accrington writes of a neighbour who specialised in getting cats up from long drops. He first put down a specially-made ladder and if the animal was reluctant to climb up he set fire to an oily rag and threw it down, and the cat came up very soon after.

Cats falling down long drop privies seemed to be a regular occurrence and Marlene Jaques of Burnley remembers her mother having to scrub a white Persian cat several times after a fall down the privy before it could sit by the fire in the evening without emitting the most terrible smell.

Ron Brown of Clayton-le-Moors remembers several people using a long stick with nails hammered into it to create a primitive ladder which cats were able to climb to safety from the long drop.

There were certainly many incidents of cats being killed by falling into long drops and occasionally even more tragic accidents occurred. Ken Spencer of Burnley pointed out to me a Coroner's report which concerned a small child falling into a long drop with fatal results.

Tommy Winsford of Leigh tells me that his grandfather was a coal miner and like most men who spend their working life underground enjoyed his country sports including pigeon racing and catching rabbits with ferrets. 'My father told me of two instances relating to our outside "trench" as we called it,' Tommy told me, 'the first concerned the old man's pigeons which he thought were the best in Lancashire. He brought a pair of birds home from his hut on his allotment tired after a training flight and they took a liking to the privy and one had the cheek to lay an egg on the seat. Convinced that he had a champion bird within the egg, the sitting bird could not be disturbed and a deal was struck with the miner next door. They agreed to share their privy in exchange for a small percentage of the winnings obtained by the "new recruit".

'The second instance concerns the antics of a particularly efficient ferret which kept the family in rabbit meat for several years. Ferrets being ferrets the animal suddenly wriggled its way out of the bag and in a trice its nose had opened the lid and it was down into the long drop in search of rats. For several days the ferret stayed there sleeping and eating. Nobody dared use the privy "for serious purposes" for fear of having their rear ends bitten and even when the ferret came home the family fear remained. The rumour started by one of the mischievous miners asserted that the ferret was a female and there was now a whole tribe of ferrets feeding on rats but had a particular liking for "plump human arses." '

Other people also seem to have had less agreeable squatters in their privy than pigeons. Donald Petty of St Helens (who was at pains to let me know that this was his real name) tells me that he had an uncle who sailed out of Liverpool and Manchester Docks. On one trip he arrived home from the sea the day before his wife's birthday and he had brought her a parrot.

To make sure that he surprised her, a friend kept the parrot for him overnight with strict instructions to put it in the privy in the early hours of the morning so that he could collect it whilst his wife was getting the breakfast.

This parrot was used to opening its own cage with its beak. Unfortunately the poor lady was taken short in the night and crept out to the privy not taking a light in case she disturbed her husband. There she was contemplating nature when the friendly parrot dropped onto her shoulder and screeched 'bugger off! bugger off!'

She did just as ordered and only began to stop shaking and see the funny side three hours later when the parrot had saluted family and friends with the same expletive!

Hubert Preston whose family once farmed near Lancaster also has a bird story but this concerns 'the other end' so to speak: 'Leading down from the long drop we had a wooden door which could be opened whilst the ash and muck were shovelled out. One day a strong wind blew the door open and our particularly aggressive cockerel entered the refuse area to strut his stuff. My father closed the door not knowing that the cockerel was fastened in.

'My little sister went to use the long drop and whilst she was occupied the cockerel flew up the long drop and fastened his talons into her bottom. We heard her screams of pain and terror from two fields away where we were working. My grandfather who had a wicked sense of humour said: "Shall us send fert doctor or t'vetinary?" In the end we settled for iodine which was almost as painful for the little mite but at least she knew what was coming!'

Eric Fordham who lived for a while outside Ormskirk worked as a railway foreman in the 1930s and his smallholding was not far from the line. As he was on his last trip of the day his mate sounded the whistle. His wife then knew it was time to get his tea ready. One day he arrived home to find no tea and no wife. He went to the neighbour's and then to the shops and only as a last resort did he go down to his allotment. There he saw his billy goat banging its head against the privy door. At the risk of life and limb he 'ticed the billy away with a bunch of carrots. He released the terrified lady who showed him that his neighbour's fence and the privy door had almost been destroyed. The reason for this was not too far to seek – the neighbour had just bought a nanny goat in the hope that the two would get together and he could sell the result of the union. Peace was restored soon after and Eric's tea was thereafter on time and for many years goat's cheese was on the menu!

Eric also told me that the staff of country railway stations never minded emptying their privy buckets because there were competitions for the best kept gardens with good prizes often on offer. Little side areas hidden away were used to grow vegetables, but the platforms were always a riot of colour in the summer with sweet-smelling tea roses planted close to the privies. This tradition was kept up even when flushing systems were introduced.

A 'shy correspondent' from Southport told me that her 'pet fear' when going to the privy was that she would be bitten by a rat. 'Imagine my fear when my father discovered that the wooden privy seat had been badly chewed in the night. Knowing of my fear dad kept watch and three nights later he discovered the culprit which was not a rat but a squirrel which had its drey in a small pine wood near our farm. In those days (1920s) red squirrels were common whereas now they are nearly extinct.'

This is quite amazing when you think our native red squirrels were once considered a pest. The American grey squirrel was not brought to England until around 1875 and they have adapted so well that they are now a pest. Walter McPherson remembers watching red squirrels breeding in a conifer plantation near the village of Worsthorne and his friend and he used to use an old privy as a hide. Their garden was long and the privy was right at the bottom and the lads, both keen naturalists in the 1920s knew the value of the lean-to shack as a hide. Still as bright as a button although nearly 90, Walter is living in retirement in Preston and can still relate the birds he watched from the long drop, recalling long tailed tits, barn owls and sparrowhawks.

Wilfred Jaques worked in a Burnley cotton mill all his life but he also took a keen interest in nature – wild rather than human in this case. Birds used to collect the flecks of cotton fibre, which seemed to float inside and outside the mills, and weave them into their nests. After coming back from holiday he found a robin had made a soft cotton nest on the seat of the privy. A neighbourhood debate took place which resulted in the family of robins taking up residence until the flight of the youngsters, 'whilst we flit next door and shared their privy.'

There are numerous accounts of hedgehogs using the warmth and comfort of privies to hibernate and Mollie Sayers who is in her late 80s remembers her mother having a painful encounter as she leaned back on the 'lav' seat much to the annoyance of Mr Hedgepig.

Mary Thelfall of Chorley wrote to tell me about a very tall thin boy, a friend of her brothers, who was good at extracting animals from long drops. 'My brother was a strong lad and one day our pet rabbit named Billy went missing. Eventually we could just see its white fur at the bottom of the toilet. My brother and the thin lad worked together. Down head first went the "thin one" whilst the "strong one" held his legs. Eventually after a struggle Billy was removed and after a good bath was none the worse for his escapade. The fame of "The Privy Protectors" spread and until the thin one put on weight the duo made a little extra pocket money mostly rescuing cats.'

In the list of the popularity stakes of 'critters in the loo' the two highest in order in Lancashire seem to be cats and spiders.

Seventy six years old Betty Wilkinson remembers that as a child 'When I used the WC I had to take my dad to stand guard round the corner of the privy which was on the busy street. He waited with much tutting and "God damn it" or "God blast it" especially if I took a long time. I was worse if I saw a cat whilst I was on the way especially if it was coming towards me. Why I was so frightened was that my uncle George told me that cats always went down the privy to die. It was not, however, the sound of dying cats which made our privy famous. One of my brothers took up singing and another was in the scout

Home to a range of wildlife, including spiders, an outdoor privy could be a scary place to visit, especially for the children. Here is a fine old double earth closet at Higher Haylot near Lancaster. (By kind permission of Lancaster City Museum.)

band playing piccolo. My dad relegated their "moaning" to the privy and the two lads practised hard for weeks until a petition from the neighbours in the street brought the symphony to an end.

'When I grew older my job was to clean the privy every Saturday. I used to arm myself with a sweeping brush to clear all the cobwebs away. Spiders loved these old privies, but I kept them at bay for many years. After a good sweep I attacked the "working surfaces" with hot water, scouring powder and carbolic soap.'

80

Pauline Gregory of Chorley also has a spidery tale: 'When I was about five years old we moved in with grandma. This was in Fleet Street and three families shared a communal privy.

'If you were only going for a short time it was not so bad but if going for a longer stay we went as a family and we had quite a pleasant sounding choir going to serenade the neighbourhood.

'To this day I have never seen bigger spiders' webs than those in that privy. No doubt the warmth of the candles and the numerous flies meant comfortable surroundings and good hunting for the spiders. The community feeling of all the neighbours in these back to back houses of old Chorley was amazing. We were all keen not only to help each other but also to make sure that our houses and privies were at least as clean as everybody else's.'

[6]

END OF THE INCONVENIENCE

When I first started to research the present book I set out to discover existing privies and many people smiled blandly and said 'There aren't any left are there?' I now know that the answer is 'No' and 'Yes'. No, there are no long drop privies still in active use apart from in museums but many of the original buildings were later put to good use for other purposes.

Marlene Jaques of Burnley told me that her surname in French was actually used in the same way as Americans refer to the 'John'. She then went on to tell me: 'We lived in a mill worker's terraced house in the Burnley Lane area of Burnley. Apart from an impressive long drop we even had a scratch mark on the window which was made by the pole carried by the "knocker up" in the days before alarm clocks. The knocker up was paid a small weekly fee for providing this service and we also had to pay to have the long drop cleaned.

'In this neighbourhood the privy and the coal house were mostly detached from the house and separated by a narrow passage. Just one or two, like ours, were attached to the house and were quite large because they incorporated this passage under the same roof.

'Our privy soon became multipurpose. It was a typical long drop and sitting there on a stormy night we were often terrified in case the tippler overturned. Another surprise which we had to adapt to was to be suddenly enveloped in steam when the washing up was being done in the house or indeed the washing of clothes in the kitchen wash basin.

'During the war the privy was specially reinforced to double as our air raid shelter. To be as comfortable as possible dad made

Marlene Jaques as a little girl with her mother on the left, photographed in front of their privy at Abel Street, Burnley in 1947. The two others were visitors from Guernsey who no doubt appreciated the use of paper squares for the first time since the war – during the German occupation of the island, newspapers were forbidden so they had had to use leaves.

a thick wooden board to cover the hole and mum made soft cushions. It was only put to the test on two occasions as the Germans preferred to bomb the engineering rather than the cotton towns.

'The privy building was a great play area for me. Out in the back street was a gas lamp set into a corner alcove of the building which had a flat top. I used to shin up the gas lamp and play on the roof. On the outside wall was an iron triangle for the reinforcement and this provided a smooth flat surface to bounce my ball against.

'Then we became posh and had an indoor three piece bathroom suite converted from the little bedroom. The privy was adapted for use as a dog kennel because we used to breed soft-tempered Alsatians. Dad fitted up an electric light and we could also use the building as a play room. Looking back I now think how unhygienic we seemed to be but kids would be kids and we were probably more immune to germs than is the modern health-conscious generation.'

Many people had a privy and coal house close together and when indoor WCs became the fashion the privy was used as extra storage and several folk wrote to me pointing out that it gave them the chance to stockpile wood and coal for the winter.

Mrs Joan Myers, now retired to Blackpool, told me of her days at Longsight in Manchester: 'On dark nights we dreaded a visit to the privy and we often went as a family and sang loudly to frighten off any visitors especially cats. Many a time I have had beasties jump over my knees and I just hope it was cats! Later on when I got married our three year old daughter created havoc. The toilet and the coal shed were together and she used to amuse herself in the small yard by building various shapes from coal. She had been playing and as my husband came home from work we sat down to tea. It was winter and as was his habit after tea and before settling down with the paper he headed off to the privy. Suddenly there was an almighty shout and a burst of language which Jimmy hardly knew never mind used! Our daughter had filled up the long drop right to the top with coal and his heavy bottom hit the pointed coal with a mighty thud. Poor Jimmy's bottom was a picture as it was black with coal, blue with bruising and red with blood! Poor Gail was never allowed to forget her dad's trip to the privy. "It could have been worse," he remarked when he had recovered, "she could have set the coal afire." '

Some of the village privies which were stone or brick built have been adapted to produce the most wonderful garden sheds. Monica Dawson of Southport told me that she now lives in the house left to her by her grandparents. The privy itself has gone and the structure has garden equipment in it, but the roses and honeysuckle which climbed around the door are still part of the scene and she still has a wonderful show of sweet peas in summer. When it was a privy the sweet peas killed the smell and they now barbecue close by so that they can still enjoy the scent.

Mrs L. Longley of Blackpool does not have such a romantic story to tell of her privy and those of us who remember long treks on freezing winter nights will know just what she means.

'As a child I lived with the other nine members of my family in a very small cottage here in Blackpool. Going to the toilet at the end of our very long back yard was awful. With us being such a large family there was always a long wait for this facility and as candles were not cheap we had to be as quick as possible.

'I remember in 1940 when the snow was so deep that my dad took ages to dig a path to the privy. It stayed freezing cold for many weeks and chapped hands, knees and chilblains were known to us all.

'The privy was a good place to play in summer but I would not go back to the old days especially as I lie in my bed after a good hot bath and a flush toilet on tap so to speak!'

In the late 1940s I remember Anthony Brass of Liverpool, then well in his 70s, who had spent some money from a legacy putting in a toilet and bathroom inside his house and converting the privy to an astronomical observatory. He put an arm chair on the seat of the privy and poked a telescope up through a neat hole which he made on the roof. How he did it I do not know but he could even swivel the instrument. I remember him saying that he first developed an interest in the moon whilst sitting on the privy. He remarked that he was an insomniac who suffered from constipation!

Another privy which was put to scientific uses during the war was described to me by Wilfred Hutchinson of Burnley. The family privy was divided into two with one part used to breed mice which were sold to the 'war office' with live consignments being sent off by train. These days we have a rather different ethical approach to the treatment of animals, but in the 1940s with some privies being used as air raid shelters to protect us from the Germans nobody asked what the mice were used for. Scrupulously accurate breeding records were kept and it was probably no accident that a member of his family became a professor of biology at a well known university.

Dennis Davidson told me of a former public loo in Blackpool which was converted to a men's hairdressers and another similar adaptation in Oswaldtwistle won an honourable mention in a *Lancashire Evening Telegraph* 'Grimewatch' competition in 1996.

Alf Tudor of Oswaldtwistle now into his 90s remembers his

This glorious cast-iron urinal in Trawden near Colne is now a Grade 2 listed building.

apprenticeship as a plumber and his father buying an ex-First World War 'Yankie Wagon' which they used to drive around demolishing privies and installing tipplers or the modern indoor WCs. 'One tippler type was called the "Liverpool Hopper" and these were very smooth. In fact these were much better because the early models of the flushers were a bloody nightmare.'

I asked Alf which items were most often dropped down the old privies and without hesitation he said 'kittens, because people left the lids up and coal and also toys because children dropped them down for the hell of it.'

Many people mentioned whitewashing their privies but Alf remembers the 1920s when some could not afford the new WCs and compromised by 'tiling the outside loos so that they looked reet posh. In the 1930s they also lashed out their hard earned cash by buying ornate toilet paper holders off us.'

I thought that all the privies of old Lancashire would now be a thing of the past, but as I started to peer around the back streets of the cotton towns I had something of a surprise.

Many were derelict especially those around mills and where there were shared facilities. Where folk had a privy to themselves they are often brightly painted, well maintained and put to use as store rooms. John Naylor of Leigh has a house with gas central heating and an en suite bathroom. His old combination of privy and coal house now houses a desk with shelves above it. John has the finest collection of old 78 records, tapes and videos devoted to Lancashire comedians that I have ever seen. George Formby, Frank Randle, Ken Dodd, Ken Platt, Arthur Askey, Ted Ray and Les Dawson are just a few and Gracie Fields, the Rochdale Nightingale, is also represented. 'Whenever I look at my bench with the recording machines on it I always think that listening to singing above the old long drop beats me singing in my bath any day' he said.

It is strange how nobody (or at least very few) lamented the passing of the privy and everyone welcomed the new indoor WCs. Alma Peers and Carole Green sent me a wonderful poem in celebration of the passing of the good old days of the privy and the final words of this rhyme are by far the best place to conclude this book which has given me so much fun.

YE OLDE COUNTRY BOG

To reach it one must leave one's hearth, go 50 yards
    down garden path,
By thorn and bramble, nettle fringed, to find the door
    perhaps unhinged,
And when inside to sit in state, to ponder and to
    meditate,
In solitude 'neath clear blue skies, closeted from prying
    eyes,
Except for cracks and knot holes wide and odd boards
    fallen off the side,
So sanctuary is found at last and peaceful interludes are
    passed.

Oh the tales of sheer delight, of how down path in
    headlong flight,
With diarrhoea on wintry night, we fled with candle
    scarce alight,
Past gooseberry bushes and apple trees with nightshirt
    flapping in the breeze,
To hammer on the door and swear on finding someone
    else was there.

But now alas, those times are gone and what's called
    progress marches on.
For on the roads along the side are sewer trenches deep
    and wide,
And little rooms all gleaming paint, replace the privies
    old and quaint,
No longer in the dead of night, beneath the moonglow's
    gentle light,
Are ancient ceremonies made, with starlight, bucket
    and with spade,
This pageantry has passed away, since modern times
    have come to stay.

But should our dreams be realised to find a place not
    modernised,
With privy as described before, 50 yards from kitchen
    door,
Don't burn it down or wreck the place – restore it to it's
    former grace.
For such antiques are very rare, collectors who have
    cash to spare,
Will pay high prices so they say and cherish it for many a
    day,
To show much better than these rhymes the
    graciousness of former times.

Those gracious times should never ever be forgotten and if this
book helps just a little to preserve them then I shall be happy.

A Privy by any Other Name

A 'certain' place
Asterroom
Aunt Jane's
Biffy
Bog
Boghouse
Bombay
Carzy
Chamber of commerce
Chamberlain pianos ('bucket
    lav')
Chuggie
Closet
Cludgie
Comfort station
Crapper box
Crapphouse
Crapping castle
Crapping kennel
Dike
Dinkum-dunnies
Doneks
Dover House
Dubs
Dubby
Duffs
Dunnakin
Dunnekin
Dunnikin
Dunnick
Dyke
Garden loo
Garderobe
Go and have a Jimmy Riddle
Go and have a Tim Tit
Going to pick the daisies
Going to see a man about a
    dog
Going to stack the tools
Going to the George
Going to the groves
Going where the wind is
    always blowing
Gong
Gong house
Heads
Here is are

Holy of holies

Home of rest

Honk

Houses of commons

House of office

Houses of parliament

Jakes

Jerry-come-tumble

Jericho

Karzi

Klondike

Knickies

Larties

Latrine

Lavatory

Little house

Loo

My aunts

Nessy

Netty

Out the back

Petty

Place of easement

Place of repose

Place of retirement

Reading room

Round-the-back

Shit-hole

Shittush

Shooting gallery

Shunkie

Slash house

The backhouse

The boggy at the bottom

The Book of Exodus

The bush

The dispensary

The dunny

The grot

The halting station Hoojy-boo (attributed to Dame Edith Evans)

The house where the emperor goes on foot

The hum

The jakers

The jampot

The japping

The John

The lats

The long drop

The opportunity

The ping-pong house

The proverbial

The Sammy

The shants

The shot-tower
The sociable
The tandem (a two holer)
The thinking house
The throne room
The watteries
The wee house
The whajucallit
Three and more seaters
Thunder box
Two seaters
Widdlehouse
Windsor Castle
'Yer Tiz'

Especially for WCs:
Adam & Eve
Chain of events
Flushes and blushes
The penny house
The plumbing
The porcelain pony
The water box
Umtag (Russian version of the WC)
Going to inspect the plumbing
The urinal
Waterloo

ACKNOWLEDGEMENTS

More than four hundred letters flooded in from readers of local newspapers in response to my request for information on the privy. I am grateful for every one of them. My thanks also to the editors of the following newspapers who gave me space so readily:

Bury Times
Accrington Observer
Chorley Guardian
West Lancashire Gazette
Lancaster Guardian
Manchester Evening News
Burnley Express
Nelson Leader
Colne Times
Clitheroe Advertiser
Liverpool Echo

Special thanks go to the *Lancashire Evening Telegraph* and the *Bolton Evening News* for whom I write a weekly column about the history and natural history of Lancashire. My regular spot on Radio Lancashire also brought in many phone calls as did a live session I did with Red Rose Radio in Preston. Listeners from GMR Manchester and Radio Merseyside were equally generous with toilet tales.

Obviously individual contributors are named but particular thanks go to regular researchers on privies, including Ken Spencer of Burnley, Lorraine Pemberton of Staining, and Ann and

Dennis Davidson of Blackpool.

I am also indebted to Dr Andrew White who gave of his time and provided some archive photographs from the collection of the Lancaster Museum Service. The same warm welcome was also given by David Chadwick of Gawthorpe Hall and Martin Robinson-Dowland at Turton Tower.